COACHING SOUP FOR THE CARTOON SOUL

NO. 2

"WILL COACH FOR FOOD"

BY GERMAINE PORCHE' AND JED NIEDERER

Aardvark Global Publishing Company, LLC

Aardvark Global Publishing Company, LLC
www.aardvarkglobalpublishing.com

Coaching Soup for the Cartoon Soul #1
Printed in the United States of America

A & A Printing
6103 Johns Road, Suite 5-6
Tampa, FL 33634
www.printshopcentral.com (813) 886-0065

First printing, December 6, 2006

Designed by Jed Niederer & Germaine Porché

Illustrations by Jed Niederer

EAGLE'S VIEW®
SYSTEMS

Touching the Future... Today™

Certified
WBENC
Women's Business Enterprise

Certif. No. 246241

ISBN 1-4276-1359-1 (Volume 2)
ISBN 1-4276-2050-7 (3 Volume Set)

Acknowledgments:

Vicki & Murphy Aucoin
Steve & Tiffinie Autio
Susan Bagyura
Drs. David & Dawn Bush
Ron & Carolyn Cambio
Diane Chappell
Tom & Pat Colucci
Dutch & Nancee Dobish
Nigel Dyer & Judy Kellie
Bruce & Jan Edwards
Stewart Esposito
Michael Fleming
Jerry & Cathy Gauche
Steven J. Hopp
Dick Huiras
Tex & Gail Johnston
Carl & Paula King

Cristin Luman
Sara Moore
Hans & Desiree Phillips
Charles & Anita Porché
Geralyn Porché
Robert Shereck & Gisèle Privé
Tyler Reeves
Terry Sierakowski
Dr. Craig Spellman
Mike Straw
Justin Temblett-Wood
Terry & Patti Trueman
Doug Upchurch
Tim & Diane Walsh
Carmen Wisenbaker
Bob & Loraine Worrell
Ted Zouzounis

Eagle's View® Systems / CoachLab® Division
1525 Lakeville Drive, Suite 127 • Kingwood, Texas 77339 • USA
www.eaglesview.com   1-888-EVSYSTM (387-9786)
281-348-9181   FAX 281-348-9164

Introduction:

COACHING SOUP displays coaching "wisdom" on the left-hand page and presents a corresponding humor attempt on the right-hand side.

For the Coach, this book serves two purposes: To provide a bullet point reminder of proven coaching principles, and to offer a 'significance buster' so that we might not take ourselves too seriously. In this fast-paced society we live in, coaches may find this format extremely useful.

For the Non-Coach, this is an informational and intentionally quirky 'inside look' at the world's fastest growing new profession: Coaching.

You may discover some unfamiliar terms. For example, we often refer to the person receiving coaching as the "Player". Unique coaching approaches and techniques are mentioned as well. Page numbers are noted where in-depth discussions about these tools can easily be found in our book, *COACH ANYONE ABOUT ANYTHING: How to Help People Succeed in Business and Life.*

The wise Coach will interview new Clients with carefully crafted questions to get to know them at more than a superficial level.

See Chapter 11, page 123 in *Coach Anyone About Anything*.

The experienced
Business Coach will
have collected a
myriad of memorable
"catch phrases" and
acronyms to help
remind Clients of
important business
principles.

Savvy Coaches welcome impromptu visits from their Players because they recognize these visits as signs of trust and confidence in their coaching.

Executive Coaches
are sometimes amazed
at their Clients'
courage and ingenuity.

The Career Coach
listens carefully for the
Player's commitment
to fulfilling
accountabilities.

See Chapter 7, page 73 in *Coach Anyone About Anything*.

Shrewd Coaches will point out the benefits of their coaching expertise from time to time to prevent Players from taking them for granted.

See Chapter 9, page 99 in *Coach Anyone About Anything*.

An important part of
the Coach's job is to
ask more of Players
than Players would
ask of themselves.

See Chapter 9, page 109 in *Coach Anyone About Anything*.

It was true. Arnold had stolen the money. But surely the authorities would forgive this one little mistake.

After all, his Coach had suggested he do something outrageous this week…

The Relationship Coach is well schooled in the latest approaches to help Clients enliven their relationships.

It is not surprising that
Players who are
committed to producing
extraordinary results will
want to be coached by
rare individuals.

Entrepreneurial Coaches depend upon referrals from appreciative Clients to expand their businesses.

See Chapter 16, page 180 in *Coach Anyone About Anything*.

The Business Coach will seldom give advice.

However, when the situation warrants advice, the Coach will give it based only upon the most rigorous of business principles.

See Chapter 4, page 41 in *Coach Anyone About Anything.*

Coaches' integrity
will allow them only to
suggest possibilities
to Players that they
would suggest to
themselves under
similar circumstances.

Coaches often marvel at the innovativity of their Small Business Owner Clients.

Erudite Coaches look for body language clues to gauge how well their coaching is being received.

See Chapter 15, page 164 in *Coach Anyone About Anything*.

29

One of the many
benefits of the
Business Coaching
Profession is that
Coaches are able to
set their own
schedules.

See Chapter 16, page 174 in *Coach Anyone About Anything.*

The success of the Business Coach is nearly always traceable to a well-conceived and well-executed marketing strategy.

See Chapter 16, page 171 in *Coach Anyone About Anything.*

About the Authors:

Germaine Porché, MSOD

Germaine specializes in working with organizations to produce performance breakthroughs in productivity and leadership. She coaches executives and groups at all levels to achieve their commitments. Germaine is a resourceful and innovative designer of consulting interventions. She is President and co-founder of Eagle's View Systems, Inc. She is co-author of _Coach Anyone About Anything: How to Help People Succeed in Business and Life._

Her 18-year consulting and coaching career has included work in the energy, manufacturing, forest products, sales, insurance, customer service, law and real estate industries. Germaine has delivered her work in the US, Canada, Europe, Indonesia and Israel. She has an outstanding history as a sales and marketing professional. Prior to entering the consulting and coaching profession, Germaine founded a realty company and built a reputation for expert knowledge and top service.

Germaine holds a Master's degree in Organizational Development (MSOD) from The American University in Washington, D.C. and the National Training Laboratories Institute (NTL). She earned a B.A. in management at Our Lady of the Lake University in San Antonio, Texas.

Germaine ran her first marathon in January 2003 and has run marathons every year since. The American Business Women's Association (ABWA) presented her with the _2003 Board Award_, for outstanding service to the Humble Artesian Chapter. Germaine was named one of the _Top Ten Businesswomen in America_ for ABWA for 2006.

Jed Niederer

Jed has led seminars and workshops for over 100,00 people in personal effectiveness, coaching, communication and leadership in the US, Canada, Europe, South America, Indonesia, India, Israel, Pakistan and Australia. He is co-author of _Coach Anyone About Anything: How to Help People Succeed in Business and Life._

His 25-year coaching and consulting career has included work in the mining, energy, manufacturing, forest products, insurance, computer and healthcare industries. A skillful program developer, Jed also provides individual coaching to executives and managers in effectiveness, leadership and coaching. He is Senior-Vice President & co-founder of Eagle's View Systems, Inc.

After earning a B.A. in Communications and Advertising from the University of Washington in Seattle, Jed entered the life insurance business, becoming a million dollar producer his first year. At age 24, he was appointed as the youngest-ever agency manager for Provident Mutual Life winning the President's Trophy in 1976. Jed holds a Chartered Life Underwriter (CLU) degree from The American College, Bryn Mawr, Pennsylvania.

34

COACHING SOUP *FOR THE* CARTOON SOUL

WATCH FOR THESE TITLES:

- NO.1 – DON'T EAT THE YELLOW SNOW
- NO.3 – NO JOB TOO SMALL, NO FEE TOO BIG
- NO.4 – COACHING IS A PRIVILEGE
- NO.5 – CAN YOU GIVE ME A CLUE?
- NO.6 – WHICH CAME FIRST, THE CHICKEN OR THE CHICKEN'S COACH?
- NO.7 – PROFOUND APPRECIATION

CoachingSoup.com

The CoachLab® Game
The Gymnasium for the Coach's Mind

New Accelerated Learning Game - Players learn proven principles, new concepts and techniques of **Coaching**.

2 to 4 Players. 45 minutes.

EaglesView.com

Listed among Amazon's Best
100 Business Books for 2003

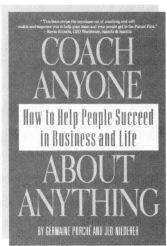

Soft Cover, 256 Pages
Retail: $16.95
ISBN 1-56912-050-1

Order online at
www.coachanyone.com
or call 281-348-9181
or 1-888-387-9786
or Fax 281-348-9164

FREE
Coaching Inventory
A self-assessment of your
Coaching Savvy
www.coachanyone.com

What Readers Say:

"*Coach Anyone About Anything* strips the mystique out of coaching and will enable and empower you to help your team get to the Future First."
— **Kevin Roberts,
CEO Worldwide, Saatchi & Saatchi**

"If you want to empower others to achieve extraordinary success, read *Coach Anyone About Anything* now!"
— **Jerry N. Gauche,
VP, Sales & Marketing,
National Oilwell Varco**

"*Coach Anyone* provides a wide variety of practical recipes for coaches to use in 'facilitating people in their own commitment and enthusiasm to accomplish their objectives'."
— **Mary Beth Moehring,
VP, Training & Organization Development,
SYSCO Corporation**

"The best coaching book on the market! The fundamentals for coaching in this book are the basis for training our new business coaches. They, and our experienced coaches, use *Coach Anyone* over and over again as the reference to serve their clients."
— **C.T. "Tex" Johnston,
CEO, Johnston Consulting Group**

"*Coach Anyone* is filled with insightful, thought-provoking ideas that apply to all walks of life. A must read for all coaches, managers, and executives."
— **David A. Stonebarger,
Director, Human Resources,
Dresser-Rand**

CoachLab® Coaching Certification Program

www.eaglesview.com
1-888-387-9786

CoachLab is a Registered Trademark ®

Ask The Coaches

The Top 10 Questions Coaches Ask About Coaching

Carmen Wisenbaker Interviews
Coaching Experts,

**Germaine Porche' and
Jed Niederer**

**In-Depth Discussions on Effective
Coaching Techniques**

CD and Workbook

AskTheCoaches.net

Quick Order Form

ONLINE: Visit www.EaglesView.com
or www.CoachAnyone.com
FAX: Send completed form to 281-348-9164
PHONE: Call 1-888-EVSYSTM (387-9786)
MAIL: Send completed form to address below

___CD/Workbook: *Top 10 Questions Coaches Ask* $19.95
___Book: *Coach Anyone About Anything* $16.95
___Cartoon Books: *Coaching Soup for the Cartoon Soul:*
    ___*#1 "Don't Eat the Yellow Snow"* $7.95
    ___*#2 "Will Coach for Food"* $7.95
    ___*#3 "No Job Too Small, No Fee Too Big"* $7.95
    ___ **All 3 Cartoon Books** $19.95
                               Subtotal $_____

Shipping: Add $3 for one item. Add $1 for each additional item ... _____
US Postal Service (<u>except</u> International: call 281-348-9181 for rates)

Sales Tax: Add 8.25% (for shipments to Texas only) .... _____

                                   Total $_____

US Funds: ___Check ___Visa ___MasterCard ___Disc ___AMEX

Card # _____ Expire Date___/___

Name on Card _____ Phone _____

Card Billing Address _____

_____

Please send more information about: ___Other Books/Products
___Speaking/Seminars ___Consulting/Coaching ___Coaching Certification
___Add me to your E-mail list for announcements, tips and techniques:

Name _____

E-Mail Address _____

Mailing Address _____ Phone _____

City _____ State/Province _____ Postal Code_____

Eagle's View® Systems / CoachLab® Division
1525 Lakeville Drive, Suite 127 • Kingwood, Texas 77339 • USA
www.eaglesview.com   1-888-EVSYSTM (387-9786)
281-348-9181   FAX 281-348-9164